A GRAPHIC HISTORY OF THE CIVIL RIGHTS MOVEMENT

MALCOLM X

AND THE FIGHT FOR AFRICAN AMERICAN UNITY

BY GARY JEFFREY
ILLUSTRATED BY EMANUELE BOCCANFUSO

Gareth Stevens
Publishing

Please visit our website, www.garethstevens.com.
For a free color catalog of all our high-quality books,
call toll free 1-800-542-2595 or fax 1-877-542-2596.

Library of Congress Cataloging-in-Publication Data

Jeffrey, Gary.
Malcolm X and the fight for African American unity / Gary Jeffrey.
p. cm. — (A graphic history of the civil rights movement)
Includes index.
ISBN 978-1-4339-7488-5 (pbk.)
ISBN 978-1-4339-7489-2 (6-pack)
ISBN 978-1-4339-7487-8 (library binding)
1. X, Malcolm, 1925-1965—Comic books, strips, etc. 2. X, Malcolm,
1925-1965—Juvenile literature. 3. African Americans—Race identity—
Comic books, strips, etc. 4. African Americans—Race identity—Juvenile
literature. 5. African Americans—Civil rights—History—20th century—
Comic books, strips, etc. 6. African Americans—Civil rights—History—
20th century—Juvenile literature. 7. Civil rights movements—United
States—History—20th century—Comic books, strips, etc. 8. Civil rights
movements—United States—History—20th century—Juvenile literature. 9.
Graphic novels. I. Title.
BP223.Z8L5747 2013
320.54'6092—dc23
2012000227

First Edition

Published in 2013 by
Gareth Stevens Publishing
111 East 14th Street, Suite 349
New York, NY 10003

Printed in China

CPSIA compliance information: Batch #DWS12GS: For further information contact Gareth Stevens, New York, New York at 1-800-542-2595.

CONTENTS

TOGETHERNESS
4

MALCOLM X AND THE FIGHT FOR
AFRICAN AMERICAN UNITY
6

"SAY IT LOUD…"
22

GLOSSARY
23

INDEX
24

The cry for African American unity was first heard loudly from Marcus Garvey in 1917. Garvey, a Jamaican-born journalist and businessman, set up the Universal Negro Improvement Association (UNIA)—the first-ever mass movement devoted to the needs of African Americans.

Marcus Garvey believed black society would only rise if it was separate from white and that black Americans should be able to go "home" to Africa.

BLACK PRIDE

One of Garvey's UNIA leaders in Omaha, Nebraska, was Earl Little. An outspoken lay preacher, Little would give powerful sermons promoting black pride. Sometimes he would bring his young son Malcolm to watch.

Earl Little's activism made him the target of racists. In Lansing, Michigan, he moved the family into a white neighborhood. Although segregation wasn't legal in the North, he had broken an unwritten rule. A white mob burned the house down.

Threats by the Ku Klux Klan drove the Little family out of Nebraska and into Michigan.

In 1931, Louise Little received the tragic news that Earl had been killed—beaten unconscious by unknown persons and laid across streetcar tracks until hit by a car. It seemed the racists had won.

YOUNG MALCOLM

Born May 19, 1925, the middle of eight children, Malcolm was light like his mom, with a sandy complexion and hair to match. In such a large family, he quickly learned how to make a noise to get attention. Following Earl's "accident," the insurance refused to pay, claiming it was suicide. Broken by misfortune, the family was split up.

Malcolm X at the height of his living fame in 1964

TEARAWAY

Although intelligent, Malcolm Little was wild at school. In 1940, he went to live with his half sister in Boston. He was 15 and into the latest styles—zoot suits and "conking" (straightening) his hair. A year later, he fetched up in Harlem, New York, and got involved in the criminal underworld.

Little's days swirled with thievery, gambling, women, and drug taking, until a death threat scared him back to Boston. Like so many before him, he seemed destined for a short, violent life as an angry young hoodlum, until one day fate stepped in…

Harlem, New York, in the 1940s

5

Malcolm X and the Fight for African American Unity

PRISON WAS HARD FOR LITTLE AT FIRST AS THE EFFECTS OF HIS ADDICTIONS WORE OFF.

HE CURSED AGAINST RELIGION SO BADLY THAT THE OTHER INMATES CALLED HIM **SATAN**.

BUT SLOWLY, HE SETTLED DOWN AND EVEN STARTED EDUCATING HIMSELF THROUGH BOOKS. HE ALSO BEGAN GETTING LETTERS FROM HIS BROTHER REGINALD...

"MALCOLM, STOP EATING PORK AND SMOKING CIGARETTES. I WILL TELL YOU HOW TO GET OUT OF PRISON..."

ALRIGHT, I CAN DO THAT IF IT'LL GET ME OUT OF HERE.

REGINALD HAD JOINED A RELIGIOUS GROUP CALLED **THE NATION OF ISLAM** (N.O.I.).

WHEN REGINALD CAME TO VISIT, MALCOLM SAID RIGHT OUT HE WASN'T INTERESTED IN RELIGION, BUT HE **DID** WANT TO KNOW HOW TO GET OUT OF PRISON...

...NOT **THIS** PLACE, MALCOLM. THE **REAL** PRISON.

YOUR **BRAIN-WASHED** MIND.

WE BELIEVE THE WHITE MAN IS **THE DEVIL.**

THINK ABOUT IT. IN ALL YOUR DEALINGS WITH THE WHITE PEOPLE, HAS ANY OF THEM EVER DONE YOU ANY **GOOD?**

LITTLE JOINED THE NATION OF ISLAM AND CONTINUED EDUCATING HIMSELF IN PRISON. WHEN RELEASED ON PAROLE IN 1952, THE FIRST THING HE DID WAS BUY SOME **GLASSES, A SUITCASE,** AND...

...FOR MY **NEW** LIFE. I'M GOING TO **SEE** MORE, **TRAVEL,** AND...

...A WRISTWATCH.

...*SEIZE* THE TIME.

HE ALSO CHANGED HIS NAME TO MALCOLM X. ONE DAY THE NATION WOULD GIVE HIM A NEW NAME, AN *ISLAMIC* NAME.

THE N.O.I. HAD BEEN FOUNDED IN 1929. ITS CURRENT LEADER WAS ELIJAH MUHAMMAD, WHOSE FOLLOWERS REGARDED HIM AS A PROPHET AND WORSHIPPED HIM ACCORDINGLY.

MALCOLM X HAD WRITTEN MANY LETTERS TO MUHAMMAD FROM PRISON AND WAS GIVEN THE TASK OF RECRUITING NEW FOLLOWERS.

GO AFTER THE YOUNG PEOPLE. **BRING THEM IN!**

MALCOLM PROVED A BRILLIANT RECRUITER AND WAS REWARDED WITH THE POSITION OF MINISTER IN TEMPLE NUMBER SEVEN IN HARLEM, WHERE HE WENT "FISHING FOR SOULS"...

WE'RE **NOT** AMERICANS, WE'RE **AFRICANS** WHO HAPPEN TO **BE** IN AMERICA. WE WERE **KIDNAPPED** AND BROUGHT HERE **AGAINST** OUR WILL FROM **AFRICA.**

WE DIDN'T **LAND** ON PLYMOUTH ROCK. THAT ROCK LANDED ON **US!**

MALCOLM'S FIERY SPEECHES WERE POPULAR, BUT OUTSIDE THE N.O.I. AND HARLEM, HE WAS STILL **UNKNOWN.**

THAT CHANGED IN 1957, WHEN A MEMBER OF TEMPLE SEVEN TRIED TO STOP A BLACK MAN GETTING BEATEN BY NEW YORK POLICE AND WAS HIMSELF ASSAULTED.

ALL HE SAID WAS, "THIS ISN'T ALABAMA."

MALCOLM LED HUNDREDS OF HIS FOLLOWERS IN A PROTEST MARCH TO THE POLICE STATION.

THE POLICE INSIDE WERE NERVOUS...

BREAK OUT THE GUNS. THERE'S GOING TO BE A RIOT!

WHEN HE TOURED WEST AFRICA, HE WAS PULLED UP OVER HIS USE OF THE WORD "NEGRO."

WE FIND THE TERM "AFRO-AMERICAN" HAS MORE DIGNITY AND MEANING.

I WILL USE THAT FROM NOW ON.

HE RETURNED DETERMINED TO PROMOTE...

...A PAN-AFRICAN UNITY THROUGHOUT ALL BLACK PEOPLES.

MALCOLM X'S CIVIL RIGHTS VISION WAS EVOLVING, BUT TIME WAS RUNNING OUT.

ON FEBRUARY 21, 1965, MALCOLM X, HIS WIFE, AND FOUR DAUGHTERS ARRIVED AT THE AUDUBON BALLROOM IN HARLEM.

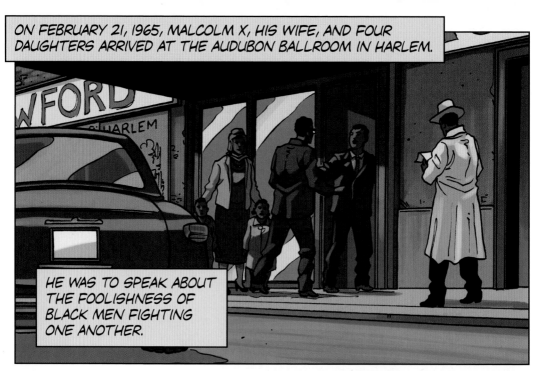

HE WAS TO SPEAK ABOUT THE FOOLISHNESS OF BLACK MEN FIGHTING ONE ANOTHER.

BUT THE SPEECH WAS INTERRUPTED BY A COMMOTION AT THE BACK.

SOMEONE'S LET OFF A SMOKE BOMB!

GET THE EXTINGUISHER!

HOLD IT, HOLD IT, DON'T GET EXCITED...

One of the killers, a hired hitman, was captured on the street outside. Two others were identified by witnesses inside the hall and later arrested. Although both members of the Nation of Islam, they have always claimed they were innocent.

FUNERAL

After Malcolm X's death, many in the media condemned him, but to others, the civil rights movement had lost a brave and bold leader, a man who was not afraid to point out the root of racial problems in America. More than 6,000 lined the streets for his funeral.

Malcolm X and Martin Luther King Jr. met briefly in 1964. Although they had different methods, they wanted the same thing for their people—freedom.

LEGACY

Malcolm X's message of black pride, self-reliance, and self-defense inspired youth movements like the Black Panthers. His mission to restore a sense of identity and history to his downtrodden brethren runs through African American culture to this day.

His autobiography, cowritten with Alex Haley and published in 1965, has been hugely influential.

GLOSSARY

accomplices People who help someone else commit a crime.

complexion The color of a person's skin, especially the face.

forbade Prohibited, did not allow.

hoodlum A disrespectful, ill-mannered troublemaker.

parole The period after a prisoner is released when his behavior is still monitored.

pilgrimage A religious journey to a holy site.

riot A violent fight involving a large group of people.

segregation The forced separation of blacks and whites in public.

suicide Ending one's own life.

thievery Stealing.

unconscious A sleeplike state in which a person is motionless and unaware of his surroundings.

underworld Illegal activities that are kept hidden from the police and other citizens who are not involved.

zoot suits A type of suit popular during the 1930s and 1940s.

INDEX

A
Africa, 4, 13, 19
Allah, 11
assassins, 21
Audubon Ballroom, 20

B
Black Panthers, 22

G
Garvey, Marcus, 4

H
Haley, Alex, 22
Harlem, New York, 5, 13, 20
hitman, 22

J
Jarvis, Malcolm "Shorty," 7

K
Kennedy, 17
King, Martin Luther, Jr., 22
Ku Klux Klan, 4

L
Lansing, Michigan, 4
Little, Earl, 4
Little, Louise, 4

M
Mecca, 18
Muhammad, Elijah, 13, 16, 17

N
Nation of Islam (N.O.I.), 8, 11–13, 16–17, 22
"Negro," 19

O
Omaha, Nebraska, 4

P
pilgrimage, 18
Plymouth Rock, 13
prison, 8–9, 12

R
Reginald, 8, 9, 11

S
Satan, 8
Shabazz, Malik, 16
suicide, 5

T
traitor, 17

U
UNIA, 4

W
watch, 7, 12